FREE-MOTION
combinations
·········· Unlimited Quilting Designs ··········

CHRISTINA CAMELI

stashBOOKS®

an imprint of C&T Publishing

Text, photography, and artwork copyright © 2021 by Christina Cameli

Publisher: Amy Barrett-Daffin

Creative Director: Gailen Runge

Acquisitions Editor: Roxane Cerda

Managing Editor: Liz Aneloski

Editor: Karla Menaugh

Technical Editor: Debbie Rodgers

Cover/Book Designer: April Mostek

Production Coordinator: Tim Manibusan

Production Editor: Alice Mace Nakanishi

Illustrator: Christina Cameli

Photography by Christina Cameli

Published by Stash Books, an imprint of C&T Publishing, Inc.,
P.O. Box 1456, Lafayette, CA 94549

Library of Congress Cataloging-in-Publication Data

Names: Cameli, Christina, 1976- author.

Title: Free-motion combinations : unlimited quilting designs /
Christina Cameli.

Description: Lafayette, CA : Stash Books, an imprint of
C&T Publishing, 2021.

Identifiers: LCCN 2021015133 | ISBN 9781644031209 (trade paperback) |
ISBN 9781644031216 (ebook)

Subjects: LCSH: Machine quilting--Patterns. | Patchwork quilts.

Classification: LCC TT835 .C356172 2021 | DDC 746.46--dc23

LC record available at https://lccn.loc.gov/2021015133

Printed in the USA

10 9 8 7 6 5 4 3 2 1

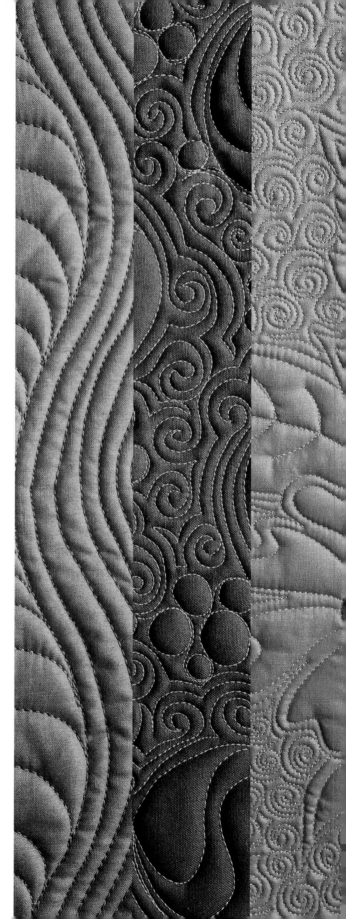

DEDICATION

To Mike, who knows the best combination has nothing to do with quilting and everything to do with family.

ACKNOWLEDGMENTS

To every quilter whose work has inspired me to look closer and to learn, thank you.

To every student who has tried something new in my class, thank you!

To my fellow PMQG members, who have woven a brilliant net of care and inspiration and togetherness, thank you.

To my children, who creatively adapted while I wrote and drew and quilted and we all ached for the end of the pandemic, thank you!

To my love, who understands what I need on a deadline more than I do, and then gracefully provides it, thank you.

To my family, who always ask about quilting and buy my fabric, even though they don't really sew, thank you.

To Karla, who has seen me through three books and takes my pet peeves seriously and makes me sound better at every turn, thank you.

To you, the person who reads the acknowledgments, for looking for what is good in the world, thank you!

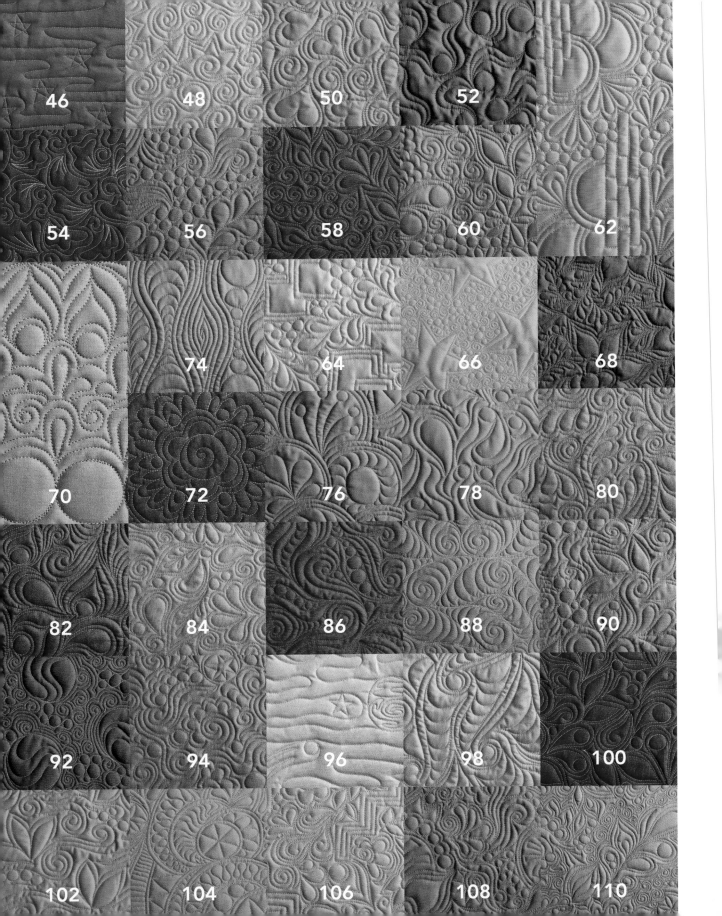

Contents

Menu of Combined Designs

OCCASIONAL VARIATIONS

Starry Night

Firecracker

46

48

ALTERNATING DESIGNS

Valentines

Ponyo

Gingko

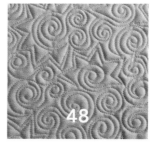

50

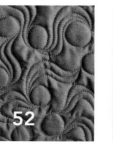

52

54

BLENDS

Fern Grove

Riverbank

56

58

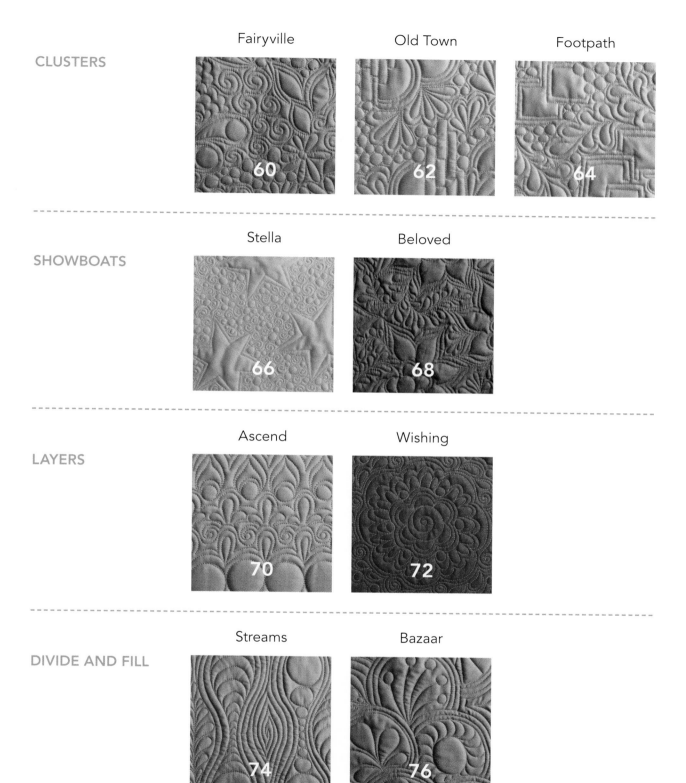

CLUSTERS

Fairyville
60

Old Town
62

Footpath
64

SHOWBOATS

Stella
66

Beloved
68

LAYERS

Ascend
70

Wishing
72

DIVIDE AND FILL

Streams
74

Bazaar
76

Splash

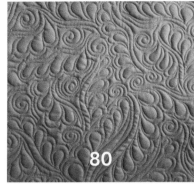

78

Midnight Garden

80

Will o' the Wisps

82

Arboretum

84

Spirit

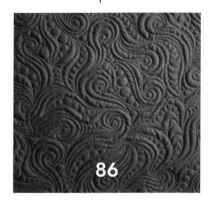

86

Fossils

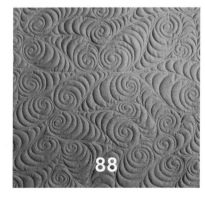

88

Floral Embrace

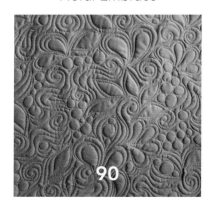

90

Bubble Town

92

Circus

94

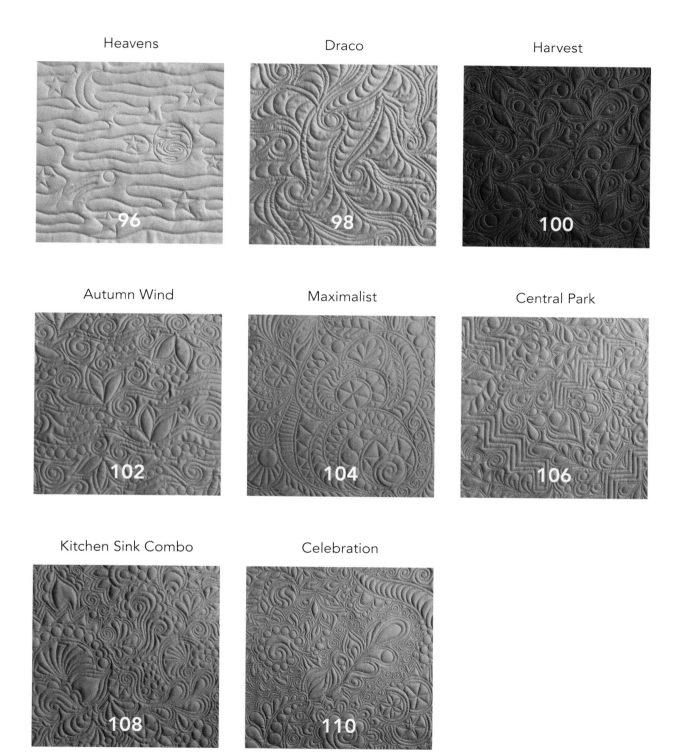

Heavens

96

Draco

98

Harvest

100

Autumn Wind

102

Maximalist

104

Central Park

106

Kitchen Sink Combo

108

Celebration

110

Introduction

As I have grown in my free-motion quilting, I have come to love combining different free-motion motifs into one piece. Designs like this are interesting to stitch and to behold. With so much detail to take in, they bring an additional layer of beauty to a finished quilt.

Working like this didn't happen overnight for me. It was the eventual result of trying one new technique at a time, drawing, quilting, puzzling, and exploring, until gradually the individual skills crystallized for me, and I was able to combine designs more fluidly and spontaneously. This makes quilting a joyful experience for me. I treasure the creative flow, as well as seeing the design unfold itself over and over until my work is done. And now I'd like to help you find your way to this quilting wonderland. I've retraced my steps so that you can join me. You can do it too!

In this book, I'll take you through a variety of approaches to combining designs. Your exploration should be equally fruitful whether you quilt sitting at a domestic machine or standing at a longarm machine. You'll discover several illustrated combinations to try yourself, and I hope you will gain a deeper understanding of how to create your own compositions using the motifs you enjoy quilting the most.

It's my hope that your quilting feels pleasurable, interesting, and uniquely yours; and that after you've done it, you feel glad for the time you spent. I hope that you will embrace little inconsistencies and imperfections as evidence of your humanity and adventurousness. Most of all, I hope that you will find continued joy in this endless, thrilling cycle of imagining, making, and learning.

Happy stitching!

Motif Library

Sometimes I need a way to remind myself of all the designs I can stitch. I made this section to be a quick reference so I don't keep stitching the same few designs on every quilt. I hope it comes in handy when you are considering what your next quilting design will be.

There is not enough space for me to show the individual steps for all of these motifs. Challenge yourself with the objective of drawing the design without lifting your pen from the paper. If you need hints, many of these motifs are explained in detail in my book *Step-by-Step Free-Motion Quilting* (page 111).

LEAVES

When leaves have complex decorations inside, I make the inner leaf shape first, then any decoration on the inside, and finally an echo around the outside.

Free-Motion Combinations

❁ FLOWERS

When stitching a complete flower, getting to the center to form all the petals can be tricky. I often do this by stitching half of a petal, moving from the outside tip to the center of the flower. I make all the other petals and then complete the last half of the first petal once I've come all the way around the flower.

Free-Motion Combinations

▮ ○ PEBBLES

When pebbles have motifs inside, I make a large pebble first and then add the decorations inside. Remember that oval or squared-off pebbles can be used too!

SPIRALS AND SWIRLS

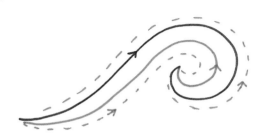

PAISLEYS

As I do with leaves, if there are motifs inside the paisley, I make a large drop shape first, then add the decorative elements inside, and finally, return to the point to echo around the outside. The only exception to this is a swirl. With this one, I make the swirl first and then add the drop shapes around it.

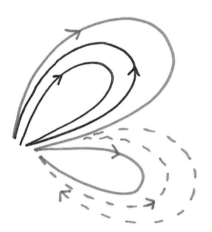

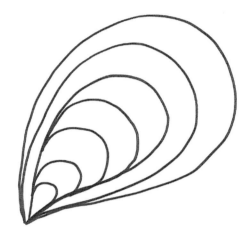

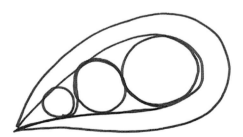

With these designs, each new motif grows off a "base": either an edge of the piecing or another motif. This means you often need to travel along the stitching of a motif you just finished to get to the place you want to start the next one. As with many other designs, make a large arc first, fill the inside, and then echo around the outside.

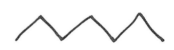

DESIGNS FOR CHANNELS

❤ OTHER MOTIFS

I left blank space on this page so you can add in motifs too!

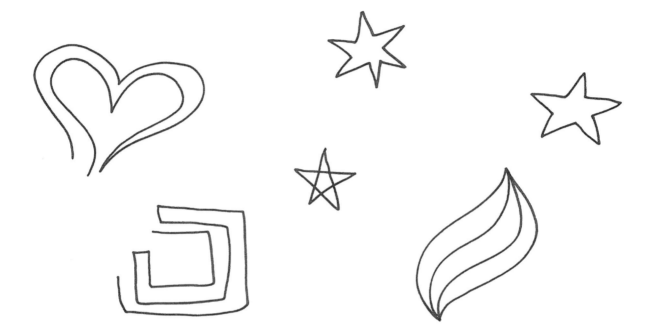

Important Allover Designs

Allover designs can be the perfect base for adding in free-motion motifs. Being comfortable with at least a few will provide you with a lot of freedom in your work. Here are the most versatile designs for quilters to use.

 SPIRALS

Turning inward, and then returning, is the easy flow of the spiral. You can easily change directions or move around the space with echoes with this design, which makes it versatile.

As you exit a spiral, you have choices about where to put the next one: right where you enter the open space (solid line), somewhere along the outside of the first spiral (long dashes), or all the way around on the other side of the first spiral (short dashes).

One thing to notice about spirals is that there are *two ways to turn* when you change directions in the middle. Notice the difference in the results. If your spirals are appearing empty to you, dive into the tight space in the center (as shown in blue), instead of immediately heading out between the curves.

WAVY MEANDERING

This is a design with a lot of flexibility, and it will be worth your time to get to know it. Gently curving lines move back and forth across the space. When the line travels off the edge, bring it back wherever it makes sense to do so. Take care to keep your spacing relatively consistent and to vary the spot where your line changes directions.

Remove the sharp points and the waves in the line, and the design is more placid.

BRANCHING DESIGNS

This is a beginner-friendly structure that allows you to complete one motif, and then start a new motif somewhere off the just-finished one. In the illustration below, I've numbered the individual branches so you can see how the design grew.

TO MAKE A BRANCH:

1. Make a curving line with a leaf at the end.

2. Move down the branch toward the starting point, adding leaves to either side as you go.

3. Once the branch is filled with leaves, move back up the stem and start a new branch. Repeat.

PAISLEYS

Paisleys are drop shapes built around one another in a back-and-forth motion. Each new one emerges from between others. Notice the open spaces (in red) where a few paisleys come together. This is normal! Don't fight it. You can always add another layer of your paisley to get to the side you want to be on (in blue).

Remember that you don't need to echo paisleys the same number of times each time. If you want to get to the other side of your paisley, just echo it again! To avoid paisleys that grow in a straight line, change direction by curving the motif as soon as you have completed 4 or so.

PEBBLES

Pebbles are just little round shapes all nestled together. When you complete one, travel at least part way around it to get to an open spot for starting the next pebble. Notice the open spaces (in red) where a few pebbles come together. You don't need to fill those spaces, it's just what happens when round shapes come together. This is geometry!

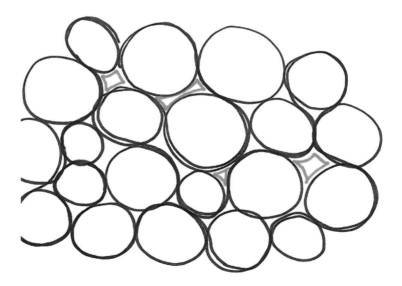

Essential Skills

Understanding these skills will improve your free-motion results no matter what design you are stitching. Take some time to absorb these messages and you'll be more comfortable as you create your designs.

LISTENING TO YOUR INTUITION

There is no more important skill for any artist than working with the creative suggestions that bubble up within you. Becoming aware of these fresh ideas takes some practice, and learning to follow them does too. You will hear me say "you'll know when" or "whenever it feels right," and I mean it. Listen to your instincts and trust them; it's an excellent act of self-love and respect, and it makes for the best quilting too. Honor your inner artistic voice and see what you create!

ECHOING

Echoing increases the texture in your work. It can make a motif more defined and noticeable. In a lot of cases, a mediocre-looking motif becomes impressive with the simple act of echoing. See where you can add echoing such as in these three motifs.

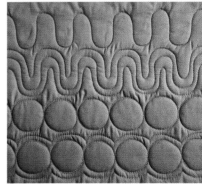

Echoing these designs made them look better!

Echoing is also an efficient way to travel from one area to another. See how the echoes (in red) took me from one place in the design to somewhere completely different.

FOLLOWING ALONG

Being able to follow the turns of a prior stitched path as you stitch a new path will lend a fluidity to your work and give an easy rhythm to your quilting.

I call this "listening to your line." This kind of creative listening means the second line is influenced by the first, and that line influences the one after, and so on. A simple way to practice is to draw some wavy lines, one right after the other. The lines can change over time, and you should let them. But they will always be *responding* to one another. When one goes right, so does the next. A perfect echo is not the goal; the goal is a sense of flow and unity.

As I listen to my line, I find I end up in similar spaces over and over. I notice that spirals and pebbles fit nicely into places where a line curves away.

MANAGING TIGHT SPOTS

Tight spots can make you stop and think about how to quilt them. Here are my go-to strategies for when I need to fill a tight space. Pick the one that works best for your space and design.

1. Echo the shapes surrounding the tight space until the space is filled with echoes.

2. Fill the tight space with a different, small motif (pebbles are my favorite!).

3. From the innermost part of the tight space, work outward, filling the space with nested arcs.

4. Add petals around one of the edges of the space.

5. Fill the space with a zigzag line.

The more you quilt (and sketch!), the fewer awkward spaces you will create, and the less you will worry about how to fill them.

Another type of tight space I encounter frequently is corners. Here are some ideas for motifs that fit well in these spaces.

CREATING A RANDOM EFFECT

The way you make turns in the design or place elements of the design affects how natural it seems. In general, varying the placement of design elements will create a more natural effect. Avoid placing things in unintentional lines. Notice in the piece below how the turning points of the design (in blue highlight) are scattered and never directly aligned top to bottom.

TRAVELING

Stitching over something you've already stitched allows you to get where you need to go in the design without adding new unnecessary lines. This technique is used plentifully in pebbles (page 30) and barnacles (page 21). You won't always hit your line. I don't, and my stitching still looks pretty good! Be easy on yourself. And keep quilting, because that's how we improve hand-eye coordination.

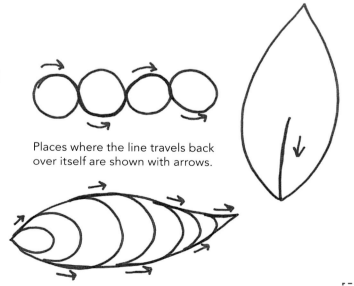

Places where the line travels back over itself are shown with arrows.

COHESION

When I quilt through my space, I try not to stray too far from the work I've already completed. If I start my next motif out in the open space, I end up leaving more hard-to-fill gaps and tight spaces, such as in the top example. In contrast, if I start new motifs right beside the already stitched area as shown in the second example, this leaves fewer open spaces to fill later.

UNDERSTANDING DENSITY

In quilted pieces, often the least-quilted area pops forward, becoming the foreground and attracting the eye of the viewer. Awareness of this is important as you put your designs together. Understanding how density affects your quilting should lead you to:

- Make the most important designs in your quilting the ones with the largest open spaces.

- Quilt more densely around anything you would like to stand out.

- Avoid leaving large unquilted areas.

- Strive for relative consistency in density across the quilt top.

To read more about these concepts, see my book *Step-by-Step Texture Quilting* (page 111).

WORKING WITHIN A DEFINED AREA

Whether it happens that you are quilting all the way to the edge of your quilt, or fitting a quilting design into a smaller area within the quilt, knowing what to do at the edges will add to your confidence. I find it helpful when stitching at the edge of the quilt to *imagine where the motif would have gone if the quilt or area was larger* and the design didn't have to end. Imagining this helps me to fill in the remaining space at the edge with a partial motif that matches the look of the whole motifs in the design.

When the design goes off the edge of the quilt, I stitch on the batting down to the point where the design would naturally continue upon the quilt surface. There, I bring the needle back onto the quilt top and continue.

For working within a smaller space on the quilt top, when I reach the edge of the space, I stitch along the edge (the "ditch" of the seamline or the previously stitched line of quilting) instead of on the batting. Practice this skill when you sketch new designs by making sure you fill your page all the way to the edge!

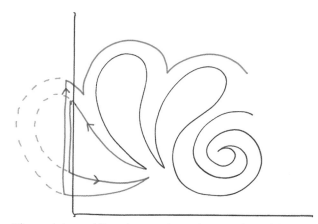

The red dotted line shows where the motif would have extended. The solid blue line shows my stitching path to complete the partial motif at the edge of the space.

FLEXIBILITY

Whatever guidelines I share here, you'll eventually need to disregard them. Maybe you're using Blends (page 40) and are facing a tight spot. You can use more or less of a motif in that round than planned to deal with the space limitations. Maybe my guidelines for a design say to echo, but you end up in a spot where there's no room to echo. You don't have to! As the quilter, you're in charge! My rules help you get started, and when you need to break them, go ahead. Seeing where you can let go of your supports is a sign of progress and mastery!

Simple Combinations

When I started on the journey of combining motifs, I did it deliberately, using specific strategies to quilt with confidence. These simple approaches are how I started. They are easy to adapt to your own style, and eventually, you may find yourself combining more than one of these strategies in the same piece.

For each approach I give you specific examples to try, but keep in mind that you can substitute *any motifs you like* and create new combinations of your own! And when you feel inspired to combine these designs, you should!

OCCASIONAL VARIATIONS

DESIGNS: Starry Night and Firecracker
(pages 46–49)

Quite possibly the simplest way to get started combining designs is to stitch an allover design that you are already comfortable with, but add in another motif occasionally. Choose any allover design, as well as a "garnish" motif. As you stitch the allover design, add in the garnish wherever it feels right. Your intuition will tell you!

ALTERNATING DESIGNS

DESIGNS: Valentines, Ponyo, and Ginkgo
(pages 50–55)

Another incredibly simple way to combine designs is to pick 2 designs, and alternate between them as you fill up the space. Stitch a single motif of the first design, then a single motif of the second design, and continue on in this pattern.

BLENDS

DESIGNS: Fern Grove and Riverbank
(pages 56–59)

Blends are similar to alternating; only instead of switching after each individual motif, you count to whatever number you choose—maybe it's one, or maybe it's more. You decide before you start how many of each different motif to make in each round, then you count them as you go.

To start, pick a few different free-motion motifs and then *decide how many of each you will stitch.* Maybe you pick 1 flower, 2 leaves, and 8 spirals.

Stitch the flower, then move on to make the 2 leaves, then the 8 spirals. Then, back to the flower, moving continuously in that order through the designs. This technique creates a consistent combination design without having to decide when to switch designs.

TIPS FOR THIS APPROACH:

- Consider making one of the motifs larger than the others.

- Have one of your motifs be a "filler" design such as pebbles, spirals, or leaves. Consider giving yourself a range to use for this one. For example, instead of limiting yourself to 10 spirals, aim for 8–14 spirals for maximum flexibility.

- Vary from your chosen recipe whenever you need to, to respond to the space you are filling.

CLUSTERS

DESIGNS: Fairyville, Old Town, and Footpath (pages 60–65)

With clusters, there is no pattern to follow. You merely *switch between designs whenever you want.* This is a great way to invite your intuition to the quilting party. Start stitching a cluster of one design, then when you feel like you've done enough of it, switch to another design. It's that simple! There's no minimum or maximum number of motifs you can repeat in a cluster.

TIPS FOR THIS APPROACH:

- Think ahead about what motifs you want to use. Once you've decided, draw the individual motifs on paper to keep nearby as you stitch. I call this a "cheat sheet" because it is a quick reference to peek at when you want to switch designs.

- Before you move on from the current design, check to see if your cluster is "blocky" (square or rectangular) in shape. If it is, expand the cluster by adding a few more of the motif until the area is less geometric. Then switch to your next motif.

- Choose motifs that look distinct from one another, either due to shape or size. Motifs that are very similar will appear to be all one motif.

- Reuse motifs whenever you like.

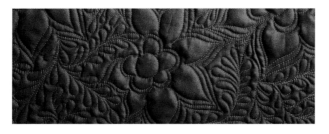

SHOWBOATS

DESIGNS: Stella and Beloved (pages 66–69)

Anytime I feature some part of my quilting prominently, I call that a *showboat*. There are dozens of ways to create showboats.

I USE THESE TWO THE MOST:

- *Echoing:* Echoing something many times will cause it to attract attention.

- *Varying the density:* Surrounding a focal motif with dense stitching allows the motif to stand out and catch the attention of the viewer.

LAYERS

DESIGNS: Ascend and Wishing (pages 70–73)

Building designs right on top of one another so that each layer responds to the layer below creates captivating geometric rhythm and movement.

I rarely use the layering technique across a whole piece, but I use it frequently as a component in my quilting. Try a flat layer in a border or a circular layer in a focal area for a mandala-like effect.

Below is a simple example of layering. A layer of arcs, then a layer of zigzags, then an echo layer.

Layering can be as simple as a single layer around one motif.

Or you might create a larger composition of layers.

Be as playful as you want with your layers. A layer (such as the spiral below) could have a single motif instead of repeating motifs. Or a layer could change from one side of a piece to another.

A layer can grow from nothing or shrink away.

DIVIDE AND FILL

DESIGNS: Streams and Bazaar (pages 74–76)

Breaking up your open space into distinct areas allows you to fill each area with a different design. This is a great way to get more motifs into your quilting without the motifs directly interacting and sharing space.

There are unlimited options for dividing the space. When I divide my space, I make sure to *echo the dividing lines* for greater definition and texture.

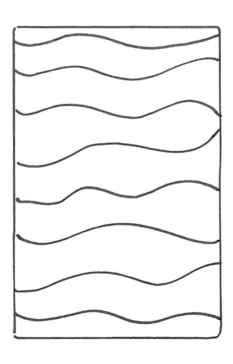

STARRY NIGHT

1. Use the allover design Wavy Meandering (page 27). Keep the wavy meandering flat, with curved direction changes.

2. Occasionally add in a five-pointed star. Start the stars from the top point.

3. Keep the stars scattered around the piece. Place a star or two on each long horizontal line.

FIRECRACKER

1. Use the allover design Spirals (page 26).

2. Occasionally, place a layer of zigzags around the outer curve of a larger spiral.

3. Echo the zigzag, then continue on with the allover design. Keep the zigzag large to help it stand out from the spirals.

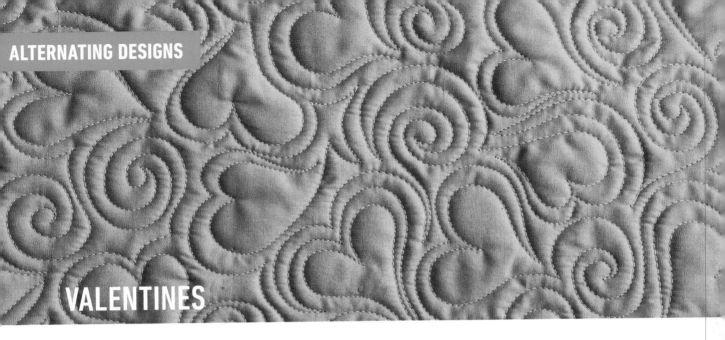

VALENTINES

1. Stitch a single spiral.

2. Stitch a heart shape. Echo it once or more.

3. Repeat the pattern. Echo whenever needed to fill in space or move around the area. Let hearts be oriented in all directions and curve when they need to.

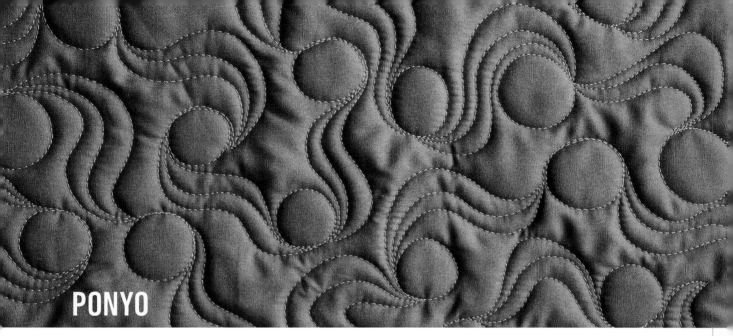

PONYO

1. Stitch a circle.

2. Leading off from the circle, make a wiggling line.

3. Echo the wiggled line back to its start and again to its end.

4. Repeat the pattern.

GINKGO

1. Stitch a curl and echo it.

2. Make a wavy-ended leaf.

3. Place some curving lines in the center of the leaf.

4. Exit from the stem of the leaf. Echo the leaf if needed.

5. Repeat the pattern.

FERN GROVE

2 CURLS: Use a long curl, starting from the bottom (uncurved) end. Echo it 3 times, until you are back at the starting point.

1 LEAFY BRANCH: Use a long stem with a drop at the end. Place drops to either side of the stem, moving downward, until you are back at the starting point, then echo around the whole motif.

7–12 PEBBLES: Feel free to use individual pebbles in any space that needs filling.

RIVERBANK

3 LEAVES: Make an open drop shape, then place a curving pointed leaf around it. Echo the leaf once or more.

1 BLOOM: Make 4 open drop shapes, fanned out, then echo around the entire motif.

7–9 SPIRALS

Free-Motion Combinations

FAIRYVILLE

The Leaves and Paisleys are the largest ingredients in this design.

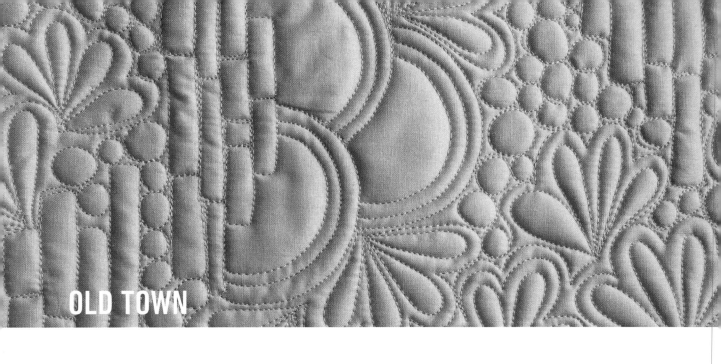

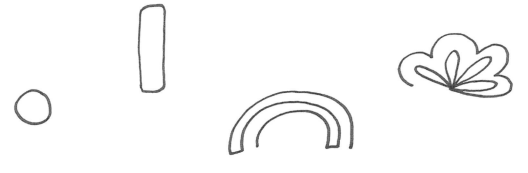

When placing a cluster of rectangular pebbles, arrange them so they are all oriented vertically, in a narrow cluster. These make an excellent base for the echoed arcs.

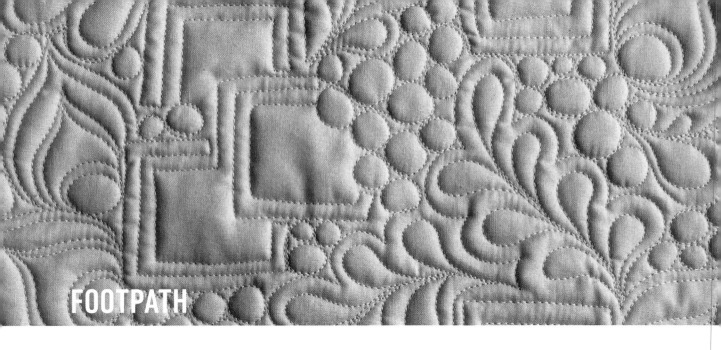

FOOTPATH

Notice how the echoed squares often grow around the corners of other squares.

Every shape in the fancy leaf is echoed for effect.

STELLA

I start this design by marking where I want my stars to be. Once I have reached a star point with my background filler, I stop and stitch the star and its echo, then continue on with the filler.

1. Make a large six-pointed star and echo it.

2. Work around the space with a combination of spirals and pebbles.

BELOVED

In this design, echoes are reserved for the flowery showboat. Use a branching design with drop-shaped leaves (page 28) for the filler.

1. Start with a tight curl.

2. Place arcs around the curl, and echo them.

3. Place leaves around the arcs, and echo at least twice more.

4. Surround the flower with the branching design, then start a new flower.

ASCEND

1. Stitch a line of pebbles.

2. Echo back across the pebbles, placing a drop shape in each depression between the pebbles. Then echo across the entire layer again.

3. Place a spiral between each drop shape, echoing over the drop shapes as you come to them.

4. Place a spray of 3 drop shapes between each spiral, echoing over the spirals as you come to them.

5. Echo over the last layer once, then begin placing flames between the sprays. Build flames with a single pebble. Echo over it once, then place a leaf shape on top of that, and a final leaf shape. Echo over the prior layer as you come to it.

6. Work from flame point to flame point with a downward pointing "V" shape that echoes itself twice.

WISHING

1. Stitch a spiral, starting from the center.

2. Add 6 arcs around the outside. Echo once.

3. Echo again, placing a pebble in each depression.

4. Add tall arcs between and over pebbles, then echo over them.

5. Make wide arcs that span 2–3 tall arcs (plan this out so you don't end up with a partial arc).

6. Echo around the wide arcs, placing a spiral in each depression.

7. Echo around the spirals, placing 2 leaning drop shapes between spirals.

8. Echo around the whole piece, placing a pebble in each depression, then echo again.

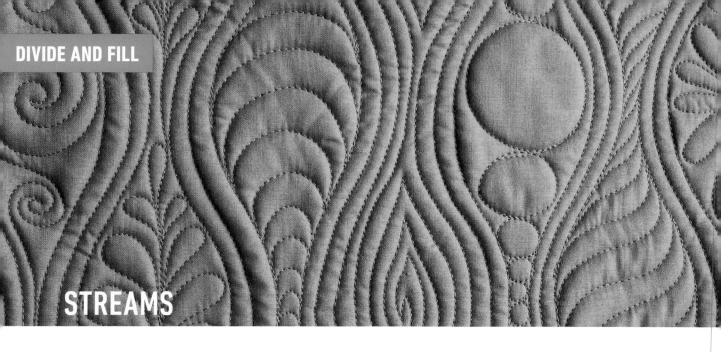

DIVIDE AND FILL

STREAMS

1. Make an undulating line. Echo it on either side.

2. Make a mirrored undulating line and echo it the same way.

3. Fill in between the lines with any design you like.

4. Continue on, each new curve mirroring the last.

Free-Motion Combinations

BAZAAR

1. Use a circular template to trace around. Start on the edge of the piece, with the template partially off. Stitch the circle and then echo it twice.

2. Move inside the open space of the circle and fill it any way you like.

3. Work your way out to the outer curve of the circle, using travel stitching.

4. Move along the outer curve to the point you want to start the next circle.

5. Place the template on the piece, partially over the finished area. Mark and then stitch the partial circle, then repeat the pattern.

Fancy Combinations

Although stricter structures provide comfort, letting go of rules makes room for *spontaneity and instinct*. In this chapter, you'll see a full page of the design as well as a description of the approach I used to create it.

Before you start going through these designs, let me emphasize that none of these designs worked out right for me the first time; it took time getting to know them, and I got to know them through sketching. Don't skip this step! Use a few pages of paper to sketch a new idea to make sure you understand how it fills the space. Do this before you move on to quilting. You could even trace over my illustrations to get a sense for how I built the design!

The designs in this chapter build on the skills and strategies I've identified in previous chapters. If these designs are beyond your grasp right now, spend time with the earlier concepts and you will grow into this realm just as I did.

SPLASH

Use wavy lines to create the structure and movement for this design. Use pebbles individually. Keep the drop shapes large. Echo everything, a lot.

MIDNIGHT GARDEN

1. Make a wavy line and echo back near its base.

2. Add drop shapes, building from the bottom up, all the way up the wavy line.

3. At the top, turn and echo back down the drops, then stitch a spiral. Repeat the pattern.

You can place extra spirals, echoes, or drop shapes anywhere.

WILL O' THE WISPS

This is a blend using one of each motif, stitched over and over in that order, with lots and lots of echoing around and between motifs. Use nested arcs to fill in tight spaces.

1. Stitch a fancy leaf.

2. Stitch an echoed spiral.

3. Stitch an echoed paisley.

4. Repeat the pattern.

ARBORETUM

Use the motifs singly, rather than in multiples, and echo often.

SPIRIT

Use echoed spirals and echoed waves. In the middle section of each echoed wave, add a channel filler such as nested arcs or pebbles. Echo whenever you need, pulling the ends of the echoes into the corners of the motifs. Fill in tight spaces with single pebbles or nested arcs.

FOSSILS

1. Make a spiral.

2. Extend a narrow shape which encloses the spiral at one end. The shape can be pointed or curved. Finish the shape near the spiral edge.

3. Fill the shape with nested arcs up to the end, then exit the shape, starting a new spiral.

FLORAL EMBRACE

Move between the motifs instinctually. The echoed wavy lines lend a fluidity to the design.

BUBBLE TOWN

1. Make a large circle. Place an "S" shape inside and echo it on either side.

2. Echo around the outside of the circle, adding spirals at random. Continue echoing, back and forth, echoing over the spirals when you come to them.

3. Start a new large circle wherever needed.

4. Use pebbles to fill in spaces between the echoed circles.

CIRCUS

Move between the motifs instinctually. Use layers of arcs or pebbles occasionally. Echo often. When using more than one pebble, place them in a line. Use nested arcs for tight spaces.

HEAVENS

Here, little thematic drawings are placed within the allover design Wavy Meandering (page 27) wherever desired.

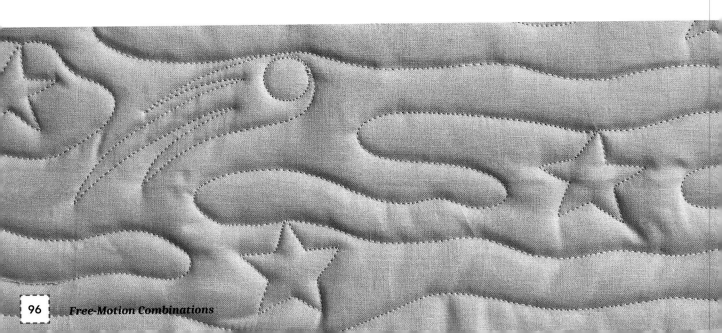

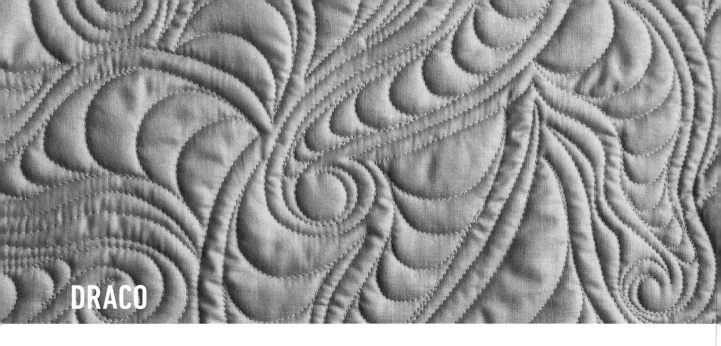

DRACO

1. Extend a long stem that leads into a spiral. Travel back along the spiral path and then break away, leaving an open space to fill.

2. Fill the space upward with nested arcs.

3. Leave the space along the edge and echo back down along that edge.

4. Echo to a place to start the pattern again.

HARVEST

Move between the motifs instinctually. Use leaves and paisleys singly or in multiples. Use blooms and pebbles singly.

AUTUMN WIND

Move between the motifs instinctually. Keep the wavy lines oriented horizontally. Leaves can be oriented in any direction. Use pebbles in a line.

MAXIMALIST

This is Divide and Fill (page 44) taken to the extreme!

1. Start with a circle. Place something inside the circle (in this case, a spiral). Return to the edge of the circle, and echo it if you like.

2. Create a large moon shape by making a nearly circular shape that starts and ends on the first circle. Fill the moon shape with a design. Work to the corner of the shape with traveling and then echo the outside of the shape.

3. Repeat Step 2 to fill the space, continually adding new shapes to the outside of the finished area, filling them and then echoing them. Use any shape you like!

CENTRAL PARK

Lightly mark the locations of your "stairways" before you start so they stay evenly distributed. When you reach an area where you want to place a stairway, make the zigzag line and then echo around it. Use any leaf, branch, or flower that comes to your mind! Once your filler designs reach where the next stairway is marked, make and echo that stairway, then continue with your other designs.

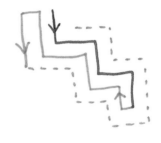

KITCHEN SINK COMBO

There are so many motifs in this design, it would fill half a page to list them all! Instead, take time to imagine my path around the piece, and notice particular techniques I used. I started here:

1. Layers (page 42)

2. Divide and Fill (page 44)

3. Clusters (page 41)

CELEBRATION

One way to make yourself a better quilter is to take in the work of other quilters and ask yourself: What do I like? What don't I like? How did they do that? Practice on this piece.

Can you find the following areas?

- Layers (page 42)
- Divide and Fill (page 44)
- Showboats (page 42)

About the Author

Photo by Lucy Glover of C&T Publishing

CHRISTINA CAMELI is an enthusiastic quilting teacher and nurse-midwife. She explores quilting with curiosity and delight. As a fabric and pattern designer she thrills at playing with color and form. As a quilter she relishes texture and spontaneity. As a teacher she loves spreading confidence and clarity. She lives with her blended family in Portland, Oregon.

Christina authored four previous books for C&T Publishing: *Step-by-Step Free-Motion Quilting*, *First Steps to Free-Motion Quilting*, *Wedge Quilt Workshop*, and *Step-by-Step Texture Quilting*.

Visit Christina online and follow on social media!

WEBSITE: christinacameli.com

FACEBOOK: /afewscraps

INSTAGRAM: @afewscraps

YOUTUBE: /afewscraps

ALSO BY CHRISTINA CAMELI: